MAKING CHILDREN'S CHOIRS WORK

by Barbara J. Mitchell
and Cheryl M. Staats

Illustrated by Diane Johnson

STANDARD PUBLISHING
Cincinnati, Ohio   3196

Scripture quotations marked (NIV) are from the Holy Bible, New International Version. Copyright © 1973, 1978. International Bible Society. Used by permission of Zondervan Bible Publishers.

Library of Congress Card No. 86-70338

ISBN 0-87403-076-5

Contents

Introduction

As directors of a youth choir, we have been surprised to find a shortage of printed material available containing practical, how-to information about beginning, building interest, and creating enthusiasm for a choir. The more we talk with leaders of other congregations, the more we realize the widespread need for a reference source that can be purchased and referred to as the directors work with their youth choirs.

Trial and error, much prayer, and a lot of hard work have enabled us to develop a description of what we feel is necessary to make an enthusiastic group of young singers for the Lord. We are filled with excitement at the potential impact on children's lives that an effective choir can make and are eager to share our ideas with others.

Our first-through sixth-grade choir, named *Kids of the Kingdom,* began several years ago. With the help of God, our pastor, and the children's parents, it has grown from an original sixteen to a current membership of forty. The children are enthusiastic, faithful in attendance, and eager to participate. They sing in worship services once a month and perform two musicals a year. In addition, they sing at local hospitals, nursing homes, other churches, and have performed on area Christian television programs. The children have learned more about God and have developed a closeness with one another. The church has increased in membership, and the community has become aware of this group of eager singers from a growing congregation.

We are thrilled to have this opportunity to share our ideas and methods of working with our group of youngsters and pray that this manual will help you to begin a choir, get some ideas to "spark" your existing group, or garner some additional tips for extra motivation. May God bless you as you invest your time and effort in helping young people learn more about His love in a special way.

Barbara and Cheryl

Growing

1
Growing

Why have a youth choir? Why spend the time, effort, and money required to make it successful? This chapter attempts to answer these questions by exploring the potential impact a youth choir can have on the lives of all involved.

Only God can see all the changes that occur as the result of a choir experience, but some areas of growth are obvious. When "Johnny-One-Note" learns to sing the melody reasonably well, it's easy to notice the difference. When "Shy Sally" stands alone for her first solo, it's a real accomplishment.

Where there is a combination of God's love, children, music, and enthusiasm, growth is bound to occur. If we keep our eyes and hearts open to see that growth, it makes all our efforts worthwhile.

Spiritual Growth

Children are influenced in many ways—by school, peer groups, and television. They eat, dress, talk, and act accordingly. It's vital that they receive positive spiritual influence as well. A children's choir program can supplement the teachings about God they learn at home and at church. As they listen and participate, they respond and learn the values proclaimed in the songs they sing. What they hear they repeat, and if they listen long enough it becomes a part of them. Singing about being "humbly grateful" rather than "grumbly hateful" can affect their reactions when problems occur. And the lyrics to a song about having patience can come to mind just when they need them most. Isn't that our main purpose in having a choir—to teach through music more about God and the change that He makes in our lives?

Children are not the only ones who become more aware of God through the lyrics they sing. Directors, too, experience spiritual growth as a direct result of working with the choir. Our lives are bound to be influenced as we teach songs about God and work with children, His "best creation." Realizing the responsibility involved in working with these young lives and the influence we could have upon the children makes us more dependent upon God for strength and guidance. There is an assurance that comes from depending on Him that diminishes our fears, and it's easy to see His handiwork even in the little things.

For example, there was a time when we were in need of nineteen sets of angel wings for a Christmas musical and found an unmarked box in the storage shed at church with ... yes, nineteen sets of wings from a Sunday-school program long forgotten. Another time funds were low and we wanted desperately to make angel dresses for the Christmas musical. Imagine our thrill when, after calling a local upholsterer for possible remnants, he supplied an extra bolt of seventy-six yards of white drapery satin—enough to make all twenty-six dresses! With renewed awareness of His love, we grew again.

Growth Through Interrelationships

Growth through interrelationships is relatively easy to see. Part of the children's enjoyment in choir comes from the friendships they develop with each other and with their directors. At the beginning of the year there may be those who are not acquainted. It's gratifying to see friendships grow in a Christian atmosphere as the year progresses.

Growth in Confidence and Ability

Standing in front of a congregation and performing is something that does not come second-nature to most of us. Children are understandably nervous the first few times they sing. But soon confidence soars as they realize what fun it can be and what positive feedback they receive as a result of their efforts. Ability, too, improves as the children practice each week. The difference in musicianship from the first of the year to the last is amazing!

God has given children abilities and talents that are sometimes untapped because we adults assume they're too young or immature. Parents have told us, for example, how little Paul wants to be in the choir but is afraid and will never be able to sing a solo or say an individual part. How surprised they are when not only does Paul sing well, but he does it all by himself in front of the entire congregation! When "everyone else is doing it," you can't hold Paul back; and in our choir we've made it a policy that "everyone does 'do it.'" It is simply expected of them, and they all know they will be given a part during the year. It doesn't matter whether each child can carry a tune or has a strong voice, for his enthusiasm can override his lack of musical ability. He doesn't know whether or not he can sing well, and his parents and church members offer nothing but praise for his efforts. With so much love and encouragement each child's confidence soars.

Growth Through Acceptance of Responsibility

In addition to gaining confidence and improving their ability to sing, members of a youth choir learn to assume responsibility—for coming to practices regularly, for their own behavior, and for learning the music. If the choir experience is positive, children will learn their music, come to practices, participate in choir activities, and sing in worship services because they enjoy it and want to be there. Each will feel he's special and know he is needed to make the group complete.

Children are the visible members of a choir. They are "out front," actively singing and participating. Parents, though not so visible, are just as vital. Those parents who initially think choir is an activity where they can send their children for an hour or so a week will soon realize that this commitment for their children is also a commitment for themselves. They will quickly get caught up in the work and planning, assume a number of responsibilities, and make new friends in the process.

Parents of our choir form a calling committee, prepare and serve refreshments at practices, make props for musicals, drive for outings, and basically do whatever is necessary to help. Without their assistance, we couldn't take on all the "extras" that help to make our program effective. The parents' willingness to do the "behind-the-scenes" work leaves us free to devote our time and attention to the children.

Growth in Numbers

An increase in the membership of a choir or a congregation is probably the easiest type of growth to see. As members of the choir bring their friends, the choir grows. As others in the community bring their children to join, attendance in worship services grows. And as children and adults hear of God's love for them, His Kingdom grows.

Growth can extend beyond the limits of a church building by acccepting invitations to sing at nursing homes, hospitals, television stations, and other churches in the community. We take our choir whenever possible, for we feel this is a way for the children to serve God and use their talents to tell others about Him. This kind of "giving experience" helps them grow spiritually, and it also helps the choir grow in number as others hear the children and want to join.

Using the local newspaper to publish articles preceding choir activities serves to create interest and also helps make the choir known in the community.

Growing in so many ways can only lead to a closer relationship with God. An active youth choir, singing and serving the Lord, can contribute to the lives of all with whom it comes in contact. But where to begin?!

Beginning

2

Beginning

What our church needs is a children's choir! Will you lead the singing? Will you play the piano?

If you've ever been asked these questions, you know the apprehension that can be felt when you accept the challenge to serve the Lord in this special way. You also know the feelings of inadequacy that can follow.

Do I know enough about music? Can I control the children? How can I make it fun and yet teach them too? Where do I start?

Directors

Qualifications for youth choir directors aren't too difficult to meet. If there were a classified ad for the job, it might read as follows:

HELP WANTED

Directors for children's choir; must have a love for God and children; some musical ability required; a sense of humor, patience, imagination, and enthusiasm essential; must be willing to work.

If you feel you meet these requirements, take on the challenge! Never underestimate your abilities when God is on your side!

Time involved in this endeavor cannot be measured just by the time it takes to select music, conduct rehearsals, or plan and present musical presentations. Therefore, we highly recommend having two directors.

The old adage, "Two heads are better than one," is certainly true when it comes to directing a children's choir. There are so many decisions to make—so many things to do—so many little individuals to love and notice! Two directors can share the responsibilities and labor as well as the blessings and fun of their choir. They can support and encourage one another. And once the two are "hooked," watch out!

Perhaps one director will take responsibility for playing the piano and one for leading the singing, but both can participate in the decision making, interaction with children,and selection of music. Sharing a choir divides the work and doubles the pleasure!

Goals, Purposes, and Objectives

If you are considering becoming a director of a children's choir, or are currently serving the Lord in this way, take a moment and visualize what you hope to accomplish. Having goals to work toward gives purpose and direction to your efforts. Don't get caught up in the routine without a vision of the potential impact a children's choir can have. Without such a vision, it's easy to become just a song leader or a piano player who puts in time with the children.

When we feed our children meat and vegetables, we are visualizing strong, healthy bodies. When we buy fluoride toothpaste, we are visualizing checkups with no cavities. Likewise, when we accept the responsibility of directing a children's choir, we also need to visualize the end result. And the end result is growth—growth in the lives of the directors, the children, and the congregation. What may start out as a little venture can grow far beyond any expectations.

16

Think through the purposes for your choir and plan objectives before the first rehearsal. Commit them to paper and refer to them frequently. Set goals, keep your heart open for God's guidance, and watch what happens! Ask questions such as

What effect will the youth choir have upon the children?
How will it benefit the congregation?
Will the choir have weekly rehearsals?
Will the children perform in worship services on a regular basis? How often?
Will the choir present a musical presentation during the year? When?
Will there be activities where the children can share their talents? What are some of them?
Will there be devotions during rehearsals?

Ages of Members

Once purposes and goals are set, the age span of the choir must be determined. Our choir is a first- through sixth-grade choir. This is quite a wide variation in age, but it works well because it combines the more mature voices of the fourth- through sixth-graders with the extra enthusiasm of the first- through third-graders. The age span of a choir will be determined, of course, by the needs and size of the congregation.

Music Selection

Anyone who watches television or listens to the radio soon realizes that music plays a vital part in the lives of young people today. From Sesame Street to the latest rock 'n roll, children listen and learn.

Christian music, too, should play a vital role in the lives of children. There is an abundance of music available in Christian bookstores, and choosing the songs to teach can be a real challenge. Songs need to be catchy and fun so they can be learned easily, yet vital and educational so they can fill children with lessons about God and His love.

When visiting a bookstore, ask to see their music selections for children. Then spend time singing or playing through the selections before you make a purchase. Many stores have facilities that allow their patrons to listen to records or tapes of the music. Don't overlook musicals as a source of music for worship services. Even if you don't intend to present the entire musical program, the songs may be perfect for your needs.

Look for songs that can be broken into individual or group solos and for which motions, sound effects, and costumes, can be used. These "extras" help get children excited about the music and give special recognition to those who participate.

Songs don't have to be slow to be meaningful. Peppy, upbeat music keeps children enthused and eager to learn. Here a choice must be made: Should your choir learn harmony and difficult scores (thereby requiring more time to be spent on each song), or should they learn more songs? We have found our children learn more lessons by learning lots of songs and oftentimes become restless spending a long time perfecting a difficult score. Since our goal is to keep them enthused and learning, we have chosen to leave the difficult scores and harmony for older choirs. The choice is up to the individual directors.

The age span of the choir, of course, sets limits on the type of music that can be used. Simple songs for little children seem logical, but even young children can learn a great deal more if they are challenged. They can repeat and learn lengthy verses if given the opportunity and if the music is catchy and the concept simple. God's creation, for example, is the theme of many songs, but children learn it best when they can croak like frogs and wave their arms like butterflies. They'll learn the deeper meanings as they mature.

Voice range, also, needs to be considered when purchasing music. We look for music with notes ranging from middle C up an octave to E, as these are most commonly in the children's range.

Identity
Get children excited right away by creating an identity

for the choir. Choose a name, theme song, logo, and colors.

Name–Children like to identify with a team. They wear their Cardinal baseball caps, cheer for the Celtics, and sing their school song. A name for the choir gives children a chance to identify with a group and instills a team spirit. Being one of the "King's Kids," "Kids of the Kingdom," or "Kids for Christ" has much more identity than just being a member of a "Junior Choir."

Theme Song–Just as a school song instills the pride of identity in its students, so a theme song instills the pride of identity in choir members. Finding a good one–one which has an upbeat, catchy tune and a meaningful message– takes time but is worth the effort. We chose Ralph Torres' "Kids of the Kingdom," and it was an instant success with both our "Kids" and our congregation. We sing it periodically in church and always use it as an introduction when we perform elsewhere.

Colors and Logo–Choir colors and a logo give recognition, and children love recognition. We chose bright red and yellow as our colors (They look wonderful in our sanctuary too.) and a yellow crown as our logo. We use the colors in decorations for parties and for posters and bulletin boards. The logo is used wherever possible to distinguish choir members (notes to parents, articles in the church newsletter). Just like the "Golden Arches" symbolize McDonald's, the crown has come to symbolize our choir wherever it is seen at our church.

Outfits–Wearing something special gives choir members a certain distinction and adds excitement to performances. Our "Kids" wear red felt sashes patterned after Boy and Girl Scout sashes over their church clothes. White felt letters are glued diagonally across the sashes to spell *Kids of the Kingdom,* and a yellow felt crown is glued at the top. The addition of plastic badges containing the logo, name of the choir and church, and child's name makes each one's sash his own. T-shirts (in choir colors) can also be purchased and stamped or silk-screened with the choir name and logo.

Sash

Badge

T-shirt

Parental Involvement

Trying to run an effective choir program alone places too great a burden on the directors and also deprives the parents of an opportunity to work for the Lord with their children. Directors who try to do it all alone can face the possibility of early burnout or, maybe even worse, of martyrdom.

If parents know there is a genuine need for help, they are usually willing to get involved. They generally make new friends and have fun in the process.

Organizing a committee or asking for chairmen to supervise individual projects takes a bit of time in the planning stage, but it is worth the effort. Several areas of involvement are given below. There are other individual needs such as folding programs and typing scripts which parents are usually willing to do as each need arises.

Telephone Committee—This committee becomes invaluable when there is a need to relay messages regarding last-minutes changes in plans, reminders, quick messages, and even for getting drivers for outings and refreshments for fellowship following musical productions. When we need to get a message to our choir members, we call the telephone chairman who relays the messages to each of the five "callers." They, in turn, each call the five or six families on their lists. The lists include the children's names, phone numbers, and their mothers' first names. Positive, cheerful voices work

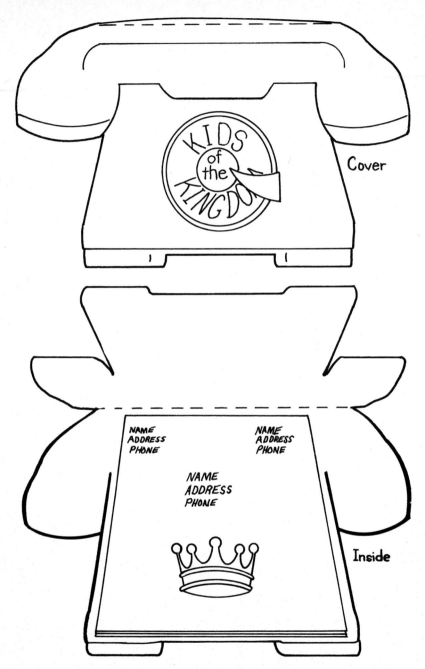

Cover

KIDS of the KINGDOM

NAME
ADDRESS
PHONE

NAME
ADDRESS
PHONE

NAME
ADDRESS
PHONE

Inside

Telephone Committee Booklet

best here, and people who feel at ease in this type of situation usually enjoy working on this committee.

Refreshment Chairman—Children need a break during choir practice if only to have an outlet for the "wiggles." Adding a small treat at this time makes it more special but can get costly and time consuming to provide week after week. Parents are usually willing to provide these refreshments if they only know when, how many, etc. A refreshment chairman can take responsibility for calling each family and setting a date when each is to bring the snack. We provide our chairman with a list of families, phone numbers, and suggested treats. These range from the traditional cookies and fruit drink to small sacks of popcorn, finger Jell-O, cereal in Styrofoam cups, or fruit. We ask that portions be small and that no seconds be given so the children can eat quickly and get back to practice. It is also helpful if parents serve and clean up after break time so the directors can be free to give special attention to the children.

Prop and Costume Helpers—Since the directors have the program books and suggestions, they usually have a good idea of what types of props and costumes are needed for specific musical productions. But having others committed to making or helping to make these items is a real blessing when the programs begin to take shape. "Work nights" where parents come to trace, cut, sew, glue, and paint, serve as a time for work and fellowship (and, of course, a way of getting the job done quickly). Parents who can't come to work can be asked if they would be willing to stop by and take some items home to complete. A deadline for returning them, though, is necessary. It helps, too, to have several parents serve on a "put-up/take-down" crew for the musicals. (Perhaps an older youth group could take on this responsibility.)

Drivers—When outings are local, it usually simplifies things to ask parents to provide transportation for their own children. When out-of-town outings are planned, however, it's necessary to get drivers and assign the children to individual cars. Careful planning here can sidestep problems before they occur. For example, a mother of one quiet first-grade girl might feel uncomfortable if assigned a car load of fifth- and sixth-grade boys. Another example, six "best friends" in one car could unintentionally ignore a seventh passenger. Grouping the children can also be a way to help a shy member make a new pal or split up a clique and let each child discover new friendships. Remind the children to buckle up and practice good safety habits. We also recommend two adults per car—one to drive and one to supervise the children.

Community Resources

There are many resources available in a community which could aid a choir. Think creatively and don't be afraid to ask. Often what some businesses think of as "scraps" can be considered "treasures" in a choir program. For example:

Newspapers—The circulation department of local newspapers will often give end rolls of unprinted newsprint free to the public. This paper can be used to cut props and patterns.

Cabinet Shops—Wood scraps and discarded items could be used for props for musicals.

Upholstery Shops—Remnants from an upholsterer are usually 72" wide and sometimes several yards long. Drapery velvet, upholstery fabrics, and window sheers make beautiful costumes!

Public Libraries—Libraries contain a wealth of information on costuming and prop designs. They are also a good source for records for background music to fit particular settings.

School Supply Stores—These stores are geared to items for working with children and contain wonderfully creative ideas just waiting to be used. Browsing through the aisles can provide numerous ideas.

Graphic Arts Departments—Often high school graphic arts departments are a good source for printing programs and badges. The students benefit from the experience, and the church benefits from the lower cost.

Furniture and Appliance Stores—Large packing boxes have multiple uses for props. They can be cut, painted, and even braced with wooden strips to be freestanding. These store flat and transport easily.

Round-Up Party

What better way to start a venture for children than with a party! A fun party planned around a definite theme (circus, western, or outer space) can create enough excitement and enthusiasm to last for a long time! VBS directors, Sunday-school teachers, and ministers are good sources for prospective members. Posters, the church paper, and personal invitations are a good way to advertise.

A party is fun but also a lot of work. Having parents help with games, prizes, and food can be a real time-saver and also a way to get them involved with the choir. Including a choir practice at the party helps the children learn right from the start that fun and work go hand-in-hand in the choir.

A sample round-up party, complete with theme, games, a design for invitations, and refreshment and prize ideas is included here. The games are simple, but it has been our experience that today's children can still enjoy simple activities if they are well planned and supervised. Once round-up invitations are mailed and the party planned, the fun is ready to begin!

ROUND-UP PARTY

Use these suggestions along with your own creative thoughts for an exciting and unique way to begin your youth choir.

Theme: Kingdom County Fair

Invitation Pattern: These are made from construction paper, assembled, and mailed to prospective members. Make a master list of names and addresses of children invited.

The inside ticket is a separate card for the children to use for admission to the fair. It is tucked in a slit cut in the back of the invitation. (See page 26.)

Decoration Ideas: Plastic-colored flags, crepe-paper streamers, multi-colored balloons

Costumes: Directors wear plastic hats with ribbons in choir colors. Colorful suspenders also add an old-fashioned, fun touch.

Music: Tape or records of circus music (Public libraries are a good source.)

Check In: When each child arrives, mark his name on the master list. Check spelling and address. Add age, grade in school, phone number, extra musical talents, and parents' first names.

Pin a name tag on each child.

Give each child a small sack for prizes.

Have children gather in a quiet place, welcome them, open with prayer, give each child a game card, and explain how to use it.

Game Card: These can be reproduced on 5" x 7" index cards. (See page 27.)

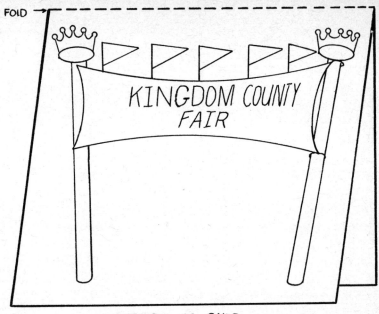

OUTSIDE OF CARD

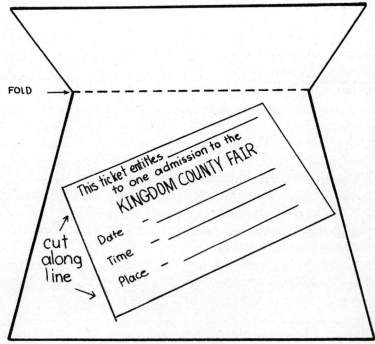

INSIDE OF CARD

KINGDOM COUNTY FAIR

1. Two Little Fishes
2. Adam and Eve
3. God Is Love
4. Bible Bookmarks
5. Jewel on the Crown
6. Cast Your Net
7. The Walls of Jericho
8. Count Your Blessings
9. Jonah and the Whale
10. Smile! God Loves You
11. My Cup Runneth Over
12. Heavenly Harvest

27

Activities: Activities in each booth are listed below. As a child goes to a booth, his game card is punched. This action is repeated at each booth until he has participated in each activity. Three of the booths will offer refreshments. Provide inexpensive prizes for every participant at the other booths (small pieces of candy, stickers, gum,or pencils). Put signs over each booth with the name of the game. Encourage the children to begin at various booths in order to minimize congestion.

(1) *Two Little Fishes:*   This game is like a fishing booth where children extend a fishing pole over a cardboard box and a helper ties a prize onto the line.

(2) *Adam and Eve:*   Use a large sheet of Styrofoam insulation as a backdrop. Make the trunk of an apple tree from brown wrapping paper. Use large sheets of construction paper for the green top of the tree. Blow up red balloons,tie the ends, and thumbtack by the ties to the tree. Children use darts (three each) to break the balloons.

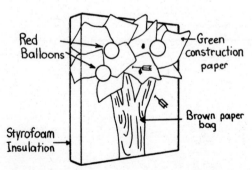

Red Balloons

Green construction paper

Brown paper bag

Styrofoam Insulation

(3) *Jonah and the Whale:*   On a large sheet of cardboard or styrofoam, draw a whale and some waves. Cut out a large mouth on the whale. Children have three tries to see if they can get a bean bag through the hole.

(4) *Bible Bookmarks:*   Obtain tongue depressors, an ink pad, and a few magic markers. Children put their thumbs onto the ink pad and decorate the tongue depressors to use as bookmarks.

(5) *Jewel on the Crown:* This game is like "Pin the Tail on the Donkey." Provide a large cardboard or Styrofoam background which contains two illustrations of a crown. Place one above the other (to accommodate different heights of children). Blindfold each child and give him a "jewel" fashioned from construction paper. Turn him around twice and let him attempt to pin (Can also use PlastiTak or a circle of masking tape on the back of the jewel.) his "jewel" on the point of the crown.

(6) *Cast Your Net:* Obtain a small kitchen strainer, a washtub, and several Ping-Pong balls. Fill the washtub partially with water and float the Ping-Pong balls. Children remove one shoe, sit on a table, hold the strainer between their toes, and "fish" for the balls.

(7) *Count Your Blessings:* Children visiting this booth write their guess for the number of items (peanuts or small candies) in a large see-through container. The child with the closest guess wins the contents of the jar at the close of the round-up party.

(8) *God Is Love:* This is a variation of a ring-toss game. Use a dowel stick for a post and make six inch rings from heavy roping or cardboard. Paint a red heart on the grass if played outdoors or on a cardboard base if played indoors. Place the dowel in the center of the heart. Give each child three tosses per turn.

(9) *The Walls of Jericho:*   Cover ten empty cans (sixteen ounces size) with brick-patterned crepe paper. Set them up in a pyramid and let children attempt to knock the cans down with a tennis ball (three tosses per turn).

(10) *Smile! God Loves You:*   This is a refreshment booth where the children receive a cupcake with a "happy face" decorated on the top.

(11) *My Cup Runneth Over:*   This is a refreshment center serving cold drinks.

(12) *Heavenly Harvest:*   This is a refreshment booth where children receive popcorn in individual plastic bags or paper cups.

———————————

Once a successful party has been conducted and children

are eager to join the choir, it's time to think about the work. Rehearsals are about to begin, and rehearsal time is valuable. It must be well planned.

A one-hour practice each week lays the foundation for the choir. It is here the choir is formed. It is here the relationships between the children and their directors are established. It is here God can be glorified through positive attitudes, Christian music, patience, love, and praise.

Children are one of God's best gifts. To help them learn about Him through music is rewarding and challenging.

But how should rehearsals be conducted? When and where should they be held?

Rehearsing

3

Rehearsing

Ah! What a delight it is to work with children in a youth choir! The children are members of the group by choice, are usually from Christian families, basically like to sing, enjoy being with their friends, and probably like the directors too. So teaching songs to these young people is an easy task.

But wait!

Jeremy just took Sue's hat ... Erin doesn't want to sit by Tammy ... Sally brought her doll to practice, and all the little girls are playing with it ... Marty spent last night with a friend and is almost asleep on the second row ... Justin just called Nicole a bad name ... No one's listening! Everyone's talking!

HELP!

THIS is the challenge for choir directors. How can a balance with discipline, fun, and learning be achieved at rehearsals? You want the children to learn the songs, have a good time, make new friends, learn more about God, and leave looking forward to next week's practice!

What a joy it would be if steps could be listed that would guarantee these results; but, unfortunately, it's not as simple as that. Maintaining discipline is an art all its own and usually a trial-and-error task.

Conducting rehearsals can be trying. However, with a little forethought, some major problems can be avoided. Anticipation is the name of the game!

Interaction — Children and Directors

Rehearsals need not be so strict that they squelch enthusiasm. Most children are made of excitement and chitter-chatter. It helps when directors can be at rehearsals a little early to listen to the adventures and mishaps that many children want to tell. Hearing about John's soccer game and Julie's hurt knee draws the directors to a closer relationship with the children. Rehearsal time goes more smoothly when these conversations take place prior to practice.

It is important to laugh and have fun. We all make mistakes as we learn. Laughing at oneself and encouraging smiles lighten and lift the spirits of children who are hesitant to sing. Praise is vital to give to the group and to individuals as often as possible. We tell our choir they are "fantastic" and remind them how much their efforts and enthusiasm are appreciated, and often how much their singing means to others.

There is a fine line between being one of the gang and being the leader of the gang. While it is important to laugh and have fun with the choir, it is also important to maintain a little distance. It may seem unrelated, but sometimes the attire of the directors determines the attitudes of the children. Teachers need to "look the part."

Rules

Too many rules make for a strict, confined rehearsal time, but no rules set the pace for a free-for-all. One suggestion is to make what we call a "Do(s) and Don't(s)" chart which can be displayed at practices and reviewed with the children as needed. When this chart is used, instead of saying, "Joe, stop pulling Erin's hair!," we can say, "Oh, Joe, *Kids of the Kingdom* DON'T pull each other's hair. We DO treat each others kindly here."

36

It may seem too easy, but it has proven to be quite an effective system. The rules on the chart are very basic ones, stated as positively as possible. When someone breaks a rule, we simply point out that members of *Kids of the Kingdom* don't behave that way. There is a sense of pride in being a good choir member—and, in the case of our choir that means following the Do(s), not the Don't(s)!

Kids of the Kingdom

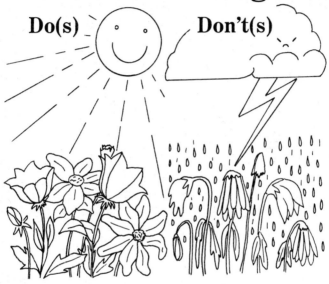

Do(s)

Don't(s)

Do sing out for Jesus.
Do behave on outings.
Do hang up their coats.
Do listen to their directors.
Do smile and have fun.
Do treat others kindly.

Don't chew gum at practice.
Don't poke, push, or shove.
Don't take hymn books out of the pews.

Policy for Absences

Attendance at practice is a touchy subject, and it's one that needs to be thought about and a policy determined for handling the familiar problem. It is important for the children to attend all the practices, for one practice builds on

37

another. Yet they and their families do have other obligations, and occasionally there are conflicts. Soccer, basketball, ballet, and piano lessons are important to their lives too. Directors need to be understanding of organized group activities, but they are justified in expecting their choir members to attend unless there is a necessary reason for their absence. The group functions best when all are present. It is helpful if parents cooperate by letting the directors know if their child will be missing a rehearsal or a performance.

It takes a little extra work, but it's important to take the time to follow up on absent members. Building on the music from week to week encourages the choir as a whole but discourages individual members who are not regular in attendance. It may be necessary to tape the rehearsals to give to the absentees so they aren't behind when they come to the next practice. Not only are the absentees better prepared the next week, but they have been reminded again how important they are to the choir.

Rehearsal Schedule

The time and day chosen for rehearsals can make or break a children's choir. Much thought is needed to determine the time of the week most suitable for both children and directors and for usage of the church building. Be forewarned, however, that no matter how hard one tries, there will never be one hour during the week that suits everyone. Children today are active, busy individuals, so choosing a time for practice is difficult. The directors, too, have many demands on their time and must evaluate their own personal life-styles to avoid conflicts with family members and outside activities. To leave home and family at a time that is inconvenient may cause stress and guilt. The directors need to be free to devote their thoughts as well as their time to the choir or the children will sense the distraction.

Once a time is established, it needs to be maintained as much as possible. If the routine is broken and practices are sporadic, the children will not establish regular patterns of attendance. This requires a real commitment on the part of directors.

Saturdays may be a day when the children are less involved in other activities. We have tried both 11:00 a.m., to noon and 1:00 to 2:00 p.m. and feel either time works well. By 11:00 a.m., the children have slept late, watched cartoons, eaten breakfast, and are usually ready to go. Practice begins on time, even if all the children are not yet there. It doesn't take long before they arrive early.

Rehearsals for our choir begin in late August and continue until the Christmas musical. Practice begins again in January and continues until the spring musical is performed the first part of May. The choir dismisses then because the children have many end-of-the-year school activities that begin to conflict with further rehearsals. (And we like to get our spring projects done at home before our children are home for the summer!)

Rehearsal Place

Choosing the best place to practice is an important consideration. Often choirs continue to meet in a particular room just because "the choir has always met there" when another room would be better. Think through the facilities and choose a location that best fills the needs of the children's choir.

Our church has a large fellowship hall, but we prefer to practice in the sanctuary because it's easier to maintain control in a quiet, reverent setting. The best piano is located there, and pews don't scoot like folding chairs! It also gives the children a chance to practice using the microphones and to become accustomed to the sound of their voices in a large room. Refreshments are served in the fellowship hall, and the change of scenery and atmosphere is a nice break.

Seating Arrangement

Personality clashes can occur in even the most congenial group of children. It's easier to handle that problem before it happens, for scolding sometimes reinforces the misbehavior. Dividing the children by classes (first- and second-graders in one row, third- and fourth-graders in another) works well because they are used to relating to each other. On the other hand, a third-grade boy may try to impress a big sixth-grader he admires and may misbehave if he sits next to him. A sweet little first-grade girl may be the darling of the sixth-grade girls, but it can cause a lot of distraction if she sits with them at practice.

Placing names on the seats and changing them weekly is another way of finding a combination of personalities and voices that works well together. This doesn't cause as much attention or distraction as having to separate children during rehearsals. It also works well as a way to help a shy, quiet child find a friend.

It also helps to have older children sitting behind younger ones so their voices can carry and help the younger ones with words and tunes.

Number of Songs Rehearsed

How many songs can be learned at a practice? How long does it take to perfect each song for a presentation? These are thoughts that need to be taken into consideration when planning rehearsals. It's better to have too many songs than too few. Just as at a birthday party it's reassuring to have one game in reserve, so it is helpful to have one extra song ready in case the children learn the others quickly.

If the plan is to sing two songs at a worship service each month, it will probably take a whole month to have them ready to perform. However, children learn fast and get bored quickly. Working on just two songs week after week would be no fun for them (or for the directors)! Variety at practices keeps choir members excited about the music and more interested in choir. It is helpful to work on three songs per week with the option of adding new ones as the old ones are polished. In that way, the choir always has a song or two in reserve for the future.

Special Parts

Some music contains three or four verses as well as a

40

chorus. It may be too time consuming to teach all four verses to the entire choir. Rather than eliminate a meaningful verse, it is helpful to give solos or duets to ease the load. This works well also if the notes or tempo are difficult for the group. The children look forward to having these special parts. They can be given to individual choir members the week before they're needed so time does not have to be taken away from the group to teach a few.

The words of the songs often determine how the parts are assigned. Lines about fish and loaves are fun for the boys to sing, while little girls enjoy singing about butterflies and flowers.

Special parts can also recapture the interest of individual children. A lack of enthusiasm, inattention, or repeated absences can be an indication that a child needs extra attention. Working with him on a solo may help.

There are ways to assign individual parts that are not sung. Children can give short introductions to the songs, a narration during a song, or recite Scripture that is applicable. Short skits can even be written to "set the stage" for the song to be presented.

For example, to introduce a song concerning working our best for God, we made up a skit about God's Employment Service, complete with personnel director and four applicants (each with an excuse for not working full-time for God).

Introductory Skit for Part-time Applications
(from the musical "What's New, Corky?")

Marc: Hear ye! Hear ye! Now taking applications for workers in God's service. Name and talent, please. (Hold large book for recording applicants.)

Kathy: I'm Kathy—I play the piano.

Shelley: My name's Shelley—I plunk a mean bass.

41

Brandy: Brandy's my name—and I love to sing (la, la, la).

Marc: Fine. God can always use good musicians. When can you work?

Kathy: All day Monday.

Shelley: Put me down for Thursdays.

Brandy: After school on Tuesdays and Wednesdays would work best for me.

Marc: Sorry. Don't call us; we'll call you. Next! Name and talent, please.

Todd: Todd—and I play soccer. (Wear uniform.)

Tom: My name's Tom—I can hit a baseball out of sight! (Wear uniform.)

Mary Kay: My name's Mary Kay—I love to race in my go-cart! (Wear helmet.)

Marc: Great! We can always use winners on our team! When can you work?

Todd: Saturday mornings are best.

Tom: Thursday afternoons for me.

Mary Kay: Friday nights after supper would be a good time.

Marc: Sorry. Don't call us; we'll call you. Next! Name and talent, please.

Michelle: My name's Michelle, and I like to smile.

Jeff: Just call me Jeff. I like to talk.

Chris: And my name's Chris. I like to read. (Carry book.)

Marc: Good! Those are all valuable talents for God's Kingdom. When can you work?

Michelle: Not in the morning! I'm too sleepy then.

Jeff: Anytime except when I'm playing with my friends.

Chris: Well, I can read my Bible on Sundays.

Marc: Sorry. Don't call us; we'll call you. (Closes application 'book.') You see, folks, when it comes to working for God
... (Music begins—opening line is "God's not taking part-time applications for Christians ...")

One of the more outlandish (and most exciting) introductions we ever used preceded a song that conveyed the message of starting each day for Jesus. As the introduction began, each of the children rested his head on the back of the pew, closed his eyes, and pretended to be asleep. A rooster's crow and an alarm clock bell woke up the children. This was followed by a young choir member playing a short melody on her flute. Two little girls (in robes, carrying stuffed teddy bears in their arms) made their way sleepily to the microphones to lead off with solos until the choir joined in the chorus. This was much more involved than usual, but there isn't a soul who participated who could ever forget the fun or the meaning of that song.

Sound Effects
Sometimes the message of a song lends itself to the use of

extra sound effects. These can be added "live" (kazoos, clapping, whistling, tambourines, drums, wood blocks, xylophones) or they can be in the form of cassette tapes. A song about Noah, for example, is a natural to be preceded or accompanied by a tape recording of thunder and rain. Many children play musical instruments and can play a verse alone or accompany the choir.

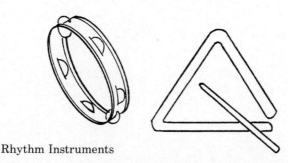

Rhythm Instruments

Rhythm instruments also can be effective and can be easily made from common, inexpensive items. Straight wooden clothespins, for example, can be used in several ways. They make a nice sound when tapped together and look cheerful when painted in choir colors. (Tied together in pairs, they have less likelihood of being dropped.) Clothespins also make a quiet bell sound when a jingle bell is attached to the top with a pipe cleaner. These props are small enough to be tucked away in pockets until needed, and the volume level does not overpower the words of the songs.

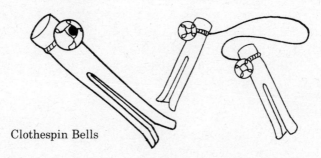

Clothespin Bells

Costumes and Props
Costumes and props add a visual reinforcement to the

messages contained in the children's songs. This is not always possible or necessary, but on occasion it provides a special touch. The children remember the song better, and they are able to convey the meaning to the congregation in an extra way.

Many songs just naturally call for visuals. They can be used by all the choir members or by just a few. For example:

A song about God's love can be made more meaningful by using white cardboard crosses with red hearts in the center to hold up each time the word "love" is sung.

A song about smiling because of God's love can have more of an impact by using yellow posterboard "happy faces" for the children to hold up each time a certain phrase is sung.

Words about trust, faith, or joy, can be grasped more clearly if the children hold up signs with those words on them.

Children basically love to role play. Adding a costume makes it fun. For example: when a song recalls Old Testament stories, children can wear "Bible-day hats," carry baskets, or have staffs. When a song pertains to thankfulness, they can wear Pilgrim collars made from paper. When a song refers to living for Jesus in every walk of life, they can wear hats to signify different occupations.

Rehearsal Routine

A set routine helps the directors include everything that is necessary at a practice and gives the children the security of knowing what to expect. Our routine is as follows: roll call, prayer, practice and explanations of songs, refreshments, recap of songs learned, and closing prayer.

Roll Call—Roll call is taken to keep track of frequent absences and to help children know their attendance is important.

Prayer—It is important to begin each session with prayer. It is a quiet time to remember why we are all there and to ask God's blessing on us as we practice for Him.

Practice and Explanations—For a number of reasons, most of them financial, we have chosen to use the rote method of teaching music to our choir. Our practice time, therefore, is spent listening and repeating phrases of the songs, then combining them until the songs are completely learned. Explanations of wording or notes are given as necessary. Most of the songs we select contain a message the children can apply to their lives, but sometimes the meaning needs to be reinforced with an explanation.

Refreshments—As mentioned in Chapter 1, parents provide and serve refreshments each Saturday for choir rehearsals. These are small portions that can be eaten quickly so children can return to the practice area. A brief change of pace like this helps in the middle of rehearsal time, and each child is proud when it's his family's turn to bring treats.

Recap—Following refreshment time, a quick recap of songs will help keep them in the children's minds until the next week.

Closing Prayer—Thanking God for the time spent at practice and praising Him ends the rehearsal on a positive note.

———————

Now that the children have practiced the songs and special parts have been learned, they are ready to have the fun of sharing them with others. But where? When? How?

Singing

4

Singing

WHERE should the choir sing?

Where there are no children singing, there are sounds of praise unsung. Their sweet, enthusiastic voices can melt the hearts of congregations; their smiles and eagerness can transform attitudes and bring joy. Children in a choir can touch the lives of those around them, and each time they do, it helps them to grow spiritually.

A choir can perform in worship services at its home church or other churches in the area, at nursing homes, hospitals, senior citizen centers, shopping malls, on religious television programs, or wherever the opportunity arises.

WHEN should the choir sing?

Whenever a youth choir sings, each child involved is making an evangelistic effort to tell others about God. If children can learn to witness in this way while they're young, it will hopefully be easier for them to share their faith when they are older. Therefore, the more opportunities they have, the better.

Children are taught in Christian homes and in Sunday-school classes to use their talents to serve God, but it's difficult for them to see concrete ways to do this. Oftentimes, young people think they have to be "all grown up" before they can be of service. A children's choir is an opportunity for children to do something special for God right now! It is an excellent place to put youthful eagerness and talents to work.

HOW should the choir present its music?

How well the choir performs depends to a great extent on how adequately it has prepared for the presentation.

Anticipation and planning are essential! Learning the music and solos is important; using visuals and costumes provides added emphasis and fun; but adequate preparation is the key to making it all work. If we expect the children to be ready, we as directors had better be ready, too!

However, even with much preparation, some things may not go as planned. Children need to know that when a mistake occurs they should just continue, smile, and have fun. Sometimes the errors are more endearing than the original, anyway.

Singing in Worship Services

Schedule—How often the children's choir sings in a worship service needs to be determined before the year begins. The schedule can be somewhat flexible to allow for holidays, revivals, etc. Overall it works well to plan to sing on a specific Sunday of each month. This provides a deadline for learning songs and gives the children many chances to perform throughout the year.

Our choir sing the second Sunday of each month. The congregation looks forward to hearing the children, and we always try to make it something special. The minister decides when he would like the choir to perform during the service, and we present the songs accordingly with the more reverent music placed closest to his message. We usually sing two and occasionally three songs. If one of the songs is extremely peppy or involves props or costumes, it is presented first. This "wakes up" the congregation and the children and gets the props out of the way before the rest of the service.

Reminders—Sending a note home with the children a week before the choir is scheduled to sing will remind parents of the exact time children should arrive at the church and relay any other special information needed. This note can be a form letter and simply filled in each month, or it can be cleverly done.

Dear Parents,

    (name of choir) will be singing _____(date)_____. They need to be at_____(place)_____ at_____(time)_____ in order to have time to line up, etc.

If your child will not be present, please call one of us so we will know in advance. Thank you.

        Sincerely,
        (Choir Leaders' names &
        phone numbers)

If notes are not used, the telephone committee can remind parents of the upcoming choir commitment.

Preparation—Most of us can remember the anticipation of seeing a filmstrip in school and the disappointment of finding the projector didn't work ... or the frustration of "seeing" a soloist perform instead of "hearing" him because the microphone was at the wrong angle or the volume wasn't set properly.

It is helpful for directors to check the microphones (height and volume) and set out any props or costumes so they will be easily accessible before the children arrive. If the choir has practiced holding up "happy faces" at a particular place in a song and the directors leave all the props in a box at home, it disappoints the children and makes it seem as if their performance is not really very important after all. If solos are practiced and ready but the microphones don't project voices, it makes the children's efforts seem wasted. If the children are ready to sing and don't know where to sit or stand to perform, "confusion" will be the message taught that day.

Because the children are usually excited the mornings they sing, it is helpful if they come about twenty minutes early. This gives them adequate time to line up and review the songs and order of service. A designated room or area helps to contain excitement and noise.

Marking each chair with the child's name will prearrange the children and give directors control of the lineup. This can change from month to month depending on soloists, behavior, and voices. If no chairs are available, masking tape strips can be placed on the floor and marked with the children's names. In this way, they will be in order and ready to go.

If there is not enough room in one area for the entire choir to assemble, individual classrooms can be used. Once again, separating the children by classes cuts down on extra commotion. (And adding an adult supervisor in each room might be a good.idea!)

Just before the children go into the sanctuary to sing is a good time to remind them what to do when they've finished.

Should they stay together in the choir loft?

Should they leave for a junior worship service?

Should they sit with their parents or with the directors?

As long as they know ahead of time what they are to do, this part should flow smoothly.

Prayer–Choir directors who seek God's guidance will feel His love and support in their endeavors. The choir members need to learn to depend on God for His help too. This lesson can be taught through example, repetition, and participation. If directors pray with the choir frequently and sincerely, the children will soon realize the importance of talking to God. They can also be encouraged to offer prayer. Beginning with prayer puts rehearsals and performances into focus.

Singing in the Community

A children's choir serves as an extension of its congregation wherever it performs. Taking God's message into the community provides a chance for evangelism and also provides good exposure for the church. When preparing for an outing, however, there are several factors to take into consideration.

(1) Is the timing right for the children (not too late at night, not too close to another performance)?

(2) Is there good access to the place where they are to perform (good place for transportation to pick up and let off the children)?

(3) Will the performance be of benefit to someone (not just busy work!)?

Once the outing is planned, there is still more work to be done.

Information—Sending a note home with each child will give the parents specific instructions concerning time, place, clothing to be worn, reminders of solos, and any other information that might be helpful or necessary. (The phone committee can relay this information instead of a note.)

Preparation—Advance work always helps, such as: check the facilities, decide the best entrance and exit of the building, locate rest rooms, take props, check microphones and sound system, determine where children will line up and stand to perform, lay out costumes.

Transportation—Transportation for an outing needs to be arranged in advance so there will be no last-minute hassles or discussions about which children ride together, and in which car. If the church has a bus or van with enough seating capacity, it can be used to transport the children. If parents are driving individual cars, the directors can provide each driver with a list of children grouped to allow for the best behavior possible. Parents may prefer to handle transportation for their own children for a local outing, and this takes away the responsibility from the directors. Stress safety.

Reminders—Taking the children aside and going over rules and expected behavior can alleviate a number of problems before they occur. A quick review of songs and solos can serve as a good reminder.

Feedback—Children love to be praised! They'll love to hear the good comments from their performances!

Presenting Musicals

Stories told with music have a way of lingering in our memories. Think of "The Sound of Music," "My Fair Lady," "Mary Poppins," "Oklahoma!" Just hearing the names of these musical classics brings vivid images to mind!

Likewise, Bible messages can be indelibly printed in the hearts of young choir members by presenting Christian musicals. The use of music, a script, costumes, and props can set the stage for one of the most rewarding and fun experiences a choir can have! Add to that the camaraderie that develops through such an undertaking and the fact that children can use this means to spread the Good News to others, and it's an irresistible opportunity.

Musicals are not for the fainthearted director, though, for they involve a great deal of work and organization. The musical has to be selected and oftentimes adapted to fit individual choirs. Parts must be divided, costumes and props made, music taught, programs prepared ... the list goes on and on. (But remember! The rewards are worth the effort!) Here are some suggestions that might help.

Selecting a Musical—There are so many musicals available in Christian bookstores and in catalogs supplied by the major publishing houses that it is difficult to choose just one! Yet there are significant differences in them. Listening to the musicals before purchasing is advisable. Many bookstores have facilities for this.

When selecting a musical, it is important to:

(1) Choose a musical with a good message or story. The choir members will remember the message taught in a musical for a long time—make it a good one!

(2) Look at it from a doctrinal point of view.Most musicals are written to be broad enough in scope to fit into the doctrines of many denominations, but it's wise to check before purchasing. Give close scrutiny to the words in the songs and script.

(3) Review songs to see if they can be taken out of context and perormed as monthly specials prior to the program. A musical score of eight to ten songs is a lot to learn in a short

period of time. Learning some of the songs ahead of time eases the pressure when it comes time to prepare for the musicals. And songs, once performed, become old friends. The children are confident when they sing them again. When practice begins for the program, efforts can be spent learning the remaining songs and adding scripts and actions.

(4) Check to be sure the characters have appropriate attitudes for the children to portray. Many programs provided by the entertainment industry have a negative connotation. Church is the place for the positive! Good musicals are a perfect medium through which children can see, feel, and participate in the Christian way of life.

(5) Pay particular attention to the music. Is it within the children's vocal range? Is it too difficult? Are there enough perky songs to make it fun? Do the songs convey meaningful themes? Are there enough solo parts? Can verses or choruses be divided to create more individual parts? Are there sections where instrumentation can be added?

(6) Look carefully at the suggestions included for staging. Are there prop and costume ideas, suggestions for adding motions to various songs, and ideas to make it flow smoothly?

(7) Notice the companion products available. Is there an accompaniment tape (or will the piano be used instead)? Is there a record or cassette? Is there a director's score?

Adapting a Musical—Many musicals are written for a few lead parts with a majority of the choir singing as a chorus. This is a very popular way of presenting a musical, and many choir directors prefer this method.

Oftentimes, though, directors would like to give individual parts to every child in the choir, but there are not enough lines or solos included in the script. Then it's time to make adaptations to the program so everyone can be included.

This is not as difficult as it may seem. For example: If the major lines are written for an elderly gentleman, a neighbor, and two children, these four characters' lines can be divided to create eight or ten individual parts. The elderly man can have a wife, there can be two neighbors instead of one, and there can be four or five children instead of two.

The same principle applies to the music. Solo parts can be divided among several children. A single verse can be sung by two soloists, two duets, or several groups of children. In fact, songs in a musical actually become easier for the choir to master when one or two of the verses are performed by soloists or small groups of children.

Dividing parts cuts down on the number of lines and solos the children must practice and memorize. That alone makes it easier for them to learn the musical. However, it also multiplies the number of children performing. That means additional movement to and from microphones, more costumes, and more organization on the directors' parts.

Assigning Parts—Children enjoy having their own lines to speak or sing in a musical. (And parents and friends like it too!) Directors have no easy task, however, when it comes to assigning special parts to their choir members. It takes time and careful strategy to involve each child in a special way. This is a good time for directors to review the individual needs of choir members. A special line may be exactly what Ann needs (even though Polly might be able to say the line more dramatically). Billy may not be the best singer in the choir, but he has wanted a solo all year. Now might be the time for him to shine! Whatever the case may be, directors need to make every child feel needed.

Rehearsing for a Musical—Rehearsing for a musical involves much more than just learning the songs. Children need to practice their speaking parts, movements on stage, use of props, and actions to songs. In order to get all this accomplished, longer rehearsals might need to be conducted for a few weeks preceding the musical. (Children often get tired of these longer practices, and it becomes difficult for directors to keep order. Plan ahead for this possibility and pray for patience!)

We hold two-hour Saturday rehearsals for approximately four weeks prior to each musical. If necessary, we have special practices (fifteen to thirty minutes) during the week for soloists, small groups, or individuals who have a lot of lines or actions to learn. Given this extra attention, the children learn very quickly. Then, at Saturday rehearsals, time doesn't have to be taken from the entire group to work with a few. The children who came during the week already know their special parts and actions, and practice flows more smoothly.

In our choir, we assign every child a special part in every musical we perform. Even though many children have only one or two lines to learn, having an individual part makes each feel special. All parts must be memorized by two weeks before the program.

During the last two rehearsals, children are placed "on stage." It is sometimes difficult to arrange choir members so all can be seen and all can see the directors during a program. One of the most valuable aids we have found to solve this problem is masking tape! A piece of tape on the floor with the child's name on it gives each his own spot and can be moved easily to rearrange children if necessary.

Movement to and from microphones, use of props, actions, and parts are practiced repeatedly during these last two rehearsals. Then it's time for the real test—dress rehearsal!

A complete dress rehearsal insures that everyone is as ready as possible. Costumes can be adjusted as necessary, microphones positioned at the proper angle and volume, and the stage set for the final performance. The musical is practiced straight through—from beginning to end. If mistakes happen, they happen. Practice continues.

Lights are turned up full for this rehearsal, and parents are encouraged to come and take pictures. We usually ask one parent to take close-ups for the choir scrapbook, and we give him a list of specific pictures to take. Usually we make a video too. Sometimes local nursing homes are invited to bring their residents to the dress rehearsals. The senior citizens can sit up close to the children and are not hindered by a crowd or dim lighting. They enjoy seeing the children, and the children try harder and behave better with an audience present.

Staging a Musical—This aspect of production may seem like an overwhelming task. Fortunately, most musicals contain staging ideas which can be adapted by directors to fit their particular needs. Here is a quick list of items to be covered.

(1) *Props*—Props and decorations don't have to be elaborate to be dramatic. Simple settings can be as effective as more elaborate ones. However, props do add color, excitement, and fun to any musical. Artistic members of the congregation may be willing to help create settings and might actually be thrilled to use their talents in this way. Parents and other members of the congregation are usually willing to help if they are made aware of the choir's needs. Whether a few props are used or whether large sets are created, a committee of willing workers is a big asset. The children will love performing when the stage is set for them.

Props are a fun part of the musicals for us. We enjoy surprising the children with as exciting a setting as we can make. We attach decorations to the walls, hang curtains on the baptistry frame, remove pews from the choir loft ... anything we can to add to the effect. Once we get started imagining, we can't seem to stop!

For *Get on Board, Children,* we lined the walls of the sanctuary with life-sized pairs of animals. These were created from colored paper and detailed by students in a graphic arts class at our local high school. The inside of the ark was illustrated on the front walls of the church by bunk beds, cages of smaller creatures, shelves of storage items, and barrels of food and grain (all made from paper).

For *Hark, the Herald Angel,* large cardboard boxes were cut to make cloud shapes. These were painted and attached to the fronts of risers so it seemed as if our "angels" were actually performing in the heavens. Stars were suspended from the ceiling beams and attached to side walls.

For *What's New, Corky?* a school setting was created in the choir loft complete with chalkboards, silhouette forms of Lincoln and Washington, alphabet cards, a "window" looking out at the playground of the "Kingdom County School" (all from paper), and the American and Christian flags.

(2) *Costumes* — It isn't necessary to costume the children for all the musicals on the market today. Many are written with the children portraying themselves, and for these the choir members can dress in their everyday clothing. But children love to wear something special, and even a small touch of costuming can create excitement. Bare feet and "freckles" were out of the ordinary and created lots of giggles when we performed *Down by the Creekbank.* When we presented *What's New, Corky?* we used hair ribbons for the girls and suspenders (dyed strips of elastic) for the boys. These fun touches required a minimum amount of effort, but the children really enjoyed them.

Investing in costumes can be like assembling a basic mix-and-match wardrobe. A few standard robes, smocks, belts, and collars can be combined to create different looks. Once these are made, they can be used again and again. With just a few touches they can be adapted to different musicals. For example: One of our most useful costumes was made from a reversible apron pattern. Members of the congregation donated used sheets which we dyed yellow. The "smocks" were made yellow on one side and white on the other. In *What's New, Corky?* the yellow side sported wide sashes with bows at the waists for the girls. But the smocks looked equally good when our boy angels wore them on the white side with sleeves attached and yellow collars and navy blue bow ties for *Hark, the Herald Angel.* These same smocks were used again over shepherds' robes to make a layered look in *Christmas 2001.* They then became Israelite soldier attire in *Miracle after Miracle* with the addition of a felt coat of arms and straps of elastic (previously suspenders) crossed in the front. These army smocks were worn over t-shirts and short pants. We gave the children cardboard shields to carry bearing the same coat of arms, and the total costume was quite effective.

Costumes

Reversible Apron

Apron
with Sash and Bow

Boy Angel

Layered Shepherd's Robe

Army Smock

Costumes can become expensive and time-consuming, but there are ways to minimize the cost. Sometimes material considered scrap by a retailer can turn into a treasure for a children's choir. Mothers and other seamstresses in a congregation might be willing to sew all the costumes.

Our choir was given remnant bolts of upholstery and drapery fabric by a local interior designer, and this donation has been the basis for most of our costumes. Because upholstery fabric is usually seventy-two inches wide, an entire costume can be made from less than one yard of fabric. (Scraps can be used for belts and collars.)

Our simple basic pattern has been sashed, belted, layered, trimmed with yarn or ribbon, worn with collars and over-jackets. We do whatever we can do to adapt it to meet the needs of the programs and sizes of the children.

Some type of a hat usually completes the look of a costume, but many times children fidget with "headgear" because it is uncomfortable. Our solution for the girls who portrayed Bible-day children was to cut the following shape from sheer drapery fabric. The straight edge was turned

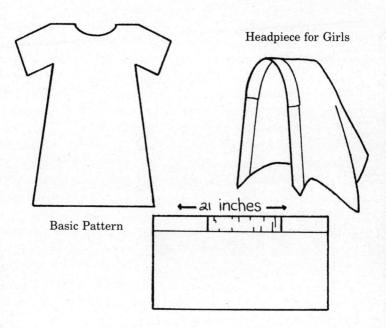

Headpiece for Girls

Basic Pattern

← 21 inches →

under, a casing made, and a headband slipped into the casing. These hats are lightweight, resist slipping, yet don't have to be tied or hair-pinned in place (and they look precious on the girls!).

It's a little more difficult to find comfortable hats for boys. Of course, the traditional towel or piece of fabric tied around the head is always effective. One additional suggestion is to buy one-half inch trim to three-fourths inch trim and make headbands with small pieces of elastic stitched in the back to allow for a snug fit. These headbands are basically comfortable and secure. When constructed from silver or gold trim, they even make good halos without looking too fancy for the Christmas productions.

Costuming ideas can be found in standard pattern books, in the costuming section of a public library, in Bible story books, children's coloring books, and (most importantly) in the imagination.

(3) *Lighting*—Single spotlights or groups of lights create special effects during a performance. They can be purchased or rented if finances permit. (It might be possible to borrow lighting from another source in the community.) Even a color wheel (from the old aluminum Christmas tree era) casts an interesting glow of color on the set.

(4) *Risers and Microphones*—No matter how good a program is, it will not be enjoyed if the audience has to strain to see and hear. Risers and microphones are a necessity.

The main reason for elevating the choir is to enable the audience to see each child as he performs. What a disappointment if a child has practiced and learned his part and then can't be seen! Conversely, risers enable the children to see the director as well. Children are easily distracted and might miss their cues if they do not have eye contact with the director.

Microphones help the children's voices project into the room. Even though children are asked to speak loudly, nothing can replace an amplifier system. Even one microphone can make a difference.

Many churches already have excellent facilities for use by their choirs; but, for those churches that do not, there are several options. Risers and microphones might not require a large outlay of money. Perhaps a carpenter in the congregation would make the risers; an individual might donate microphones if the need were known; or either item could be rented (or borrowed) from a school, theater, or another church.

We were fortunate to have been given carpeted platforms by a local firm that had discontinued those particular items. Other platforms were made by a wood craftsman in the congregation. Our amplifier was donated as a memorial for a beloved member of the congregation. God supplied our needs!

(5) *Programs*—Bulletin covers are one of the companion products offered with most musicals. These can be ordered for programs or special ones can be made. For example: when our choir performed *Down by the Creekbank,* the programs actually were paper lunch sacks with a boy and creekbank scene on one side and the program on the other. For *Back at the Creekbank,* the program was printed on the back of a large fish (cut out of construction paper by our willing mothers). These types of unique programs are fun to receive and add a personal touch to the musical. But the most exciting part of having a printed program for the children is to see their names in print!

Additional Suggestions for a Musical—Here are just a few additional ideas to make the presentation of a Christian musical even more fun.

(1) *Invitations*—Children love giving invitations to friends, teachers, and family members. These can be designed for each musical and made by the children or printed professionally. Because it's impossible to reach everyone with a special invitation, the church paper, bulletins, and local newspaper can be used to invite those who might not otherwise know about the musical. Newspapers, if contacted far enough in advance, are often willing to take pictures to accompany the articles. The more the community becomes aware of the choir and congregation, the more opportunities will arise for the choir to serve God.

(2) *Refreshments*—Serving refreshments after a program is a nice way to end the evening. These refreshments don't have to be elaborate—cookies or brownies, fruit drink, and coffee will do. Choir mothers or ladies' circles are usually willing to bake and take over kitchen duties.

It helps contain the excitement if there are tables and chairs where choir members can have quick access to their treats. The use of place cards on these tables keeps commotion to a minimum. And removing costumes first saves wear, tear, and cleaning bills!

(3) *Receiving Line*—If choir members form a receiving line following a performance, they have a chance to receive immediate reinforcement for their efforts. This gives each child a chance to hear good comments and sense the pleasure he has given to others. (They may grumble and groan, but overall the children enjoy the extra attention.)

Singing in public creates excitement, whether it's in worship services, in other areas of the community, or through the medium of a Christian musical. Enthusiasm is high at performance time. But how can directors keep this level of enthusiasm for choir throughout the year?

Kids of the Kingdom

K ids of the Kingdom are
I ndescribable! Their combination of interest and
D esire has created a wonderful group to
S ing for the Lord.

O thers have received joy
F rom hearing

T his group as they
H ave used their talents and
E nthusiasm to serve God throughout the year.

K ind and considerate, yet seldom
I nactive, they are always willing to try something
N ew. By knowing that
G od comes first and
D eciding to put
O thers before themselves, they have
M ade their lives count for Him in a special way.

Maintaining
Enthusiasm

5

Maintaining Enthusiasm

Children and directors are generally excited when choir first begins in the fall. They have fun seeing old friends again, summer activities have concluded, and the new music is challenging. Enthusiasm is usually so high it is actually hard to contain!

Around November, however, the routine of weekly rehearsals can start to weigh on both the directors and the choir. School and extracurricular activities are ususally in full swing, and the newness of choir can start to wear off.

It is a challenge to children's choir directors everywhere to keep Christian music in the lives of active young people today. When things start to lag, it's time to add a spark or two to boost morale.

There are a number of imaginative ways to create extra bursts of enthusiasm. Included in this chapter is a brief recap of previously-mentioned ideas as well as some additional suggestions. But the most important element for an enthusiastic choir is enthusiastic directors! Enthusiasm is like measles and chicken pox—it is highly contagious! You can't give it to others unless you have it yourself!

Identity—Create an identity by choosing a choir name, logo, colors and theme song. (See page 18.)

Songs—Choose up-beat, peppy, and meaningful music in an easy range. (See page 17, Music Selection.)

Costumes and Props—Add these whenever possible for extra visualization and fun. (See page 59.)

Sound Effects—Use Kazoos, tambourines, rhythm instruments, whistling, clapping, drums, musical instruments, and a vivid imagination. (See page 43.)

Musicals—Depend on them to spark interest, build self-confidence, and leave a memory that will last for years. (See page 55.)

Refreshments—Serve them quickly but faithfully every week. They mean a lot to the children. (See page 22.)

Service Projects—Take the children into the community to share their talents with others. (See page 53.)

Memorabilia—Keep scrapbooks with pictures, programs, notes, articles. Everyone loves to remember and reminisce!

Change of Pace—Change the order of practice, the seating arrangement, the place where the children practice ... whatever is necessary to fight the doldrums!

Notes to Parents—Make them informative and complete. (See page 51.)

Telephone Committee—Establish good communication and friendships among the parents by using this committee. (See page 20.)

Special Parts—Assign parts to everyone during the year so all get a chance to shine! (See page 57.)

Annual Family Picnic—Have fun with the children and their families at a potluck picnic at the end of the year. It's a time when directors can relax and play with the children without having to supervise.

Round-up Party—Make it fun for all! Include games, food, and practice! Ask the parents to assist. (See page 24.)

Publicity—Make the public aware of the choir's activities by use of the local newspaper. Ask for pictures to be taken at program time.

Program Invitations—Provide children with creative invitations to give to those "special people" in their lives—parents, neighbors, close friends.

Skits—Portray the meaning of the songs and involve individual children by writing imaginative skits. Use these occasionally as introductions to songs.

Tape Recordings—Record the children's singing on a single tape during the year. Make duplicates of the tape at the end of the year for each member to keep.

Seasonal Activities—Add new spark and the "Christian touch" to the holidays by planning activities for the choir that will offer them a chance to combine fun and giving.

Halloween

(1) *Plant a Treat*—Children receive many "treats" at the Halloween season. So one year we decided instead of one more treat for the children the "Kids" could have the fun of treating the church. A note was copied on yellow construction paper and cut out in the shape of a tulip. It read: "This is no trick . . . the Kids of the Kingdom are planting a treat

for our church. If you will bring one tulip bulb (red or yellow) on October 30, there will be forty-four beautiful flowers in the spring. We'll plant them together. It's no trick!"

Each choir member was asked to purchase one red or yellow tulip bulb (our choir colors) and bring it to rehearsal on Saturday. A space of ground was prepared in advance. Choir practice was extended by thirty minutes to allow time for a short devotion about God's creation and for the actual planting of the bulbs. Each child was excited and eager to see the flowers that next spring. What fun it was to watch the first blooms of our labor together!

(2) Go Pumpkin Caroling—Inclement weather often makes it difficult to transport children for caroling at the traditional Christmas season. So, with that in mind, we have used the Halloween holiday as a chance to spread our good cheer in the fall. The minister provided names and addresses of several senior citizens who might enjoy a visit, and we took the children "pumpkin caroling." Pumpkins were purchased and mums were donated by members of the congregation. Mothers made pumpkin-shaped sugar cookies and orange frosting. With much supervision, the pumpkins were hollowed and filled with flowers (in plastic cups). The cookies were frosted to take (Some, of course, were also eaten!), and off we went to sing and give of our "harvest." Wanting to avoid inappropriate costumes, we all dressed like hobos. We had called each senior citizen in advance to tell him we were coming; otherwise, he or she might have been surprised to see such a group singing and laughing at the front door. A tape recording was made of the piano accompaniment for the songs; and, with our battery-powered cassette recorder, we were able to sing (in tune) the cheerful songs we had prepared.

Thanksgiving

(1) *Display Choir Members' Thankfulness* – At one November practice, each child received a large turkey feather made from a different color of construction paper. Each child wrote on the feather something for which he or she was thankful and signed his or her name. The feathers made a tail when glued in place on a large construction-paper turkey. On the Sunday morning that we sang our thankful songs, our poster was on display in the foyer. As the congregation entered, they enjoyed reading what the choir members were thankful for. Our turkey wore a yellow crown (choir logo style) on his head.

(2) *Dress Like Pilgrims*—Another idea is to make pilgrim collars for the choir members from white banquet paper. Pilgrim hats can be made for both boys and girls. Or dress in complete pilgrim costume one boy and girl and have them read a Biblical introduction to the music that day.

Christmas

(1) *Present a Musical*—What can compare with the delight of seeing children telling a Christian story at Christmas? Presenting a musical is an excellent way to participate in the true meaning of Christmas.

(2) *Give a Memorable Gift*—Ornaments can be an inexpensive, personalized touch for each of the children at the holiday season. Each Christmas we design an ornament to tie in with one of the props used in the musical. A couple in our congregation cuts the ornaments from wood and paints them. We print the name of the musical, the year, and the child's name on each one. These are presented to the children following the musical. We have had many comments from parents expressing how much the children enjoy reminiscing as they put the ornaments on their trees each year.

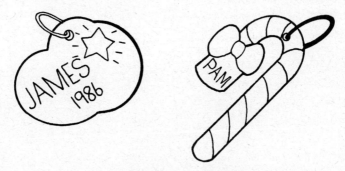

Valentine's Day

(1) *Make Valentines for the Congretation*—One February our choir decorated and handed out valentines to the entire congregation. The valentines were made at a party and contained Scriptures on love, a valentine verse, and a place for a child's signature. The children decorated the covers with hearts and doilies. The congregation was thrilled with this touch from the children, and many called the choir members to thank them or sent them valentines in return.

(2) *Make Corsages to Share*—Another Valentine's Day giving project we used was to have the children make tissue-paper flowers and present them as boutonnieres or corsages to every member of the congregation the Sunday before Valentine's Day. The Bible verse, "Love your neighbor as yourself" (Luke 10:27, NIV), was put on a tag and attached to each flower with the child's signature. The children were thrilled to look out at the congregation and see "flowers" on everyone, and the members of the church enjoyed it too.

Easter

(1) *Present a Musical*—Let the choir participate in the joy of the Easter season by presenting a musical in the spring. There are many available which are based on Bible truths, and these are especially appropriate to present at this time of the year.

(2) *Hide a Treat*—In lieu of an Easter egg hunt we asked the mother in charge of refreshments the week before Easter to do something different. We asked her to put each treat in a bag with a child's name written on the outside.

The bags were then hidden in the fellowship hall. Refreshment time was exciting that Saturday before Easter as the children searched for their refreshments.

An enthusiastic youth choir can spark a fire in the hearts of a congregation. The children can often lead their parents, as well as others, to a closer walk with God. For when the choir expresses God's love, others can feel it too.

Feeling God's Love and Care

6

Feeling God's Love and Care

Few people can describe their feelings about God's love and care for them. A personal relationship with God is just that—personal!

Christians are surrounded at all times by God's love and care, but sometimes we are made more aware of it than at others. One way to alert our senses to His presence is to give of ourselves in some area of church work.

Many people can testify to special ways that God has blessed them through their individual Christian service. For the more closely we work with someone, the better we know him. The more closely we work with God, the better we know Him. He becomes a friend, counselor, and an ever-present help.

By serving as directors of our children's choir, we have felt more attuned to God. We have seen His influence all around us. Sometimes it's been shown in quiet ways (the kind we have to look to find), like a flickering smile on a shy child's face when he learns a new song. Sometimes it's been shown in obvious ways (the kind we can't deny), like receiving a monetary donation just when our funds are running low.

God's Spirit has led us, helped us, laughed with us, and comforted us. This closeness to Him may not have developed had we not followed His leading in this endeavor.

Our hearts are filled just now with the joy of children and music and the opportunity to pass on any knowledge or experiences that might help others to share this joy. We give God the honor and glory for whatever good has come from our choir and for whatever good will come from this manual for children's choir directors.

"Give, and it will be given to you. A good measure, pressed down, shaken together and running over, will be poured into your lap. For with the measure you use, it will be measured to you," Luke 6:38 (NIV).

This is truth from God's Holy Word. And so we who love God give of ourselves—our time, our talents, our energies—to serve as His emissaries here on earth. If children can be taught early in life that giving is part of God's plan, they will have learned a valuable lesson and will hold one of the keys to true happiness.

God has given each of us talents, and we are indebted to use them to further His Kingdom. Involvement in a youth choir program is one way to put these talents to work. Youth choir directors give of their Christian influence, time, musical talents, and of their ability to work with children. Choir members give of their energies, enthusiasm, voices, laughter, smiles, and joy. Congregations give of their love and support. And all involved receive evidence of God's watchfulness and care.

"Jesus said, 'Let the little children come to me, and do not hinder them, for the kingdom of heaven belongs to such as these,'" Matthew 19:14 (NIV).

God wants children to feel the atmosphere of warmth and

love that a church can provide. A children's choir is one way to bring young people into the church programs where they can be nurtured in His teachings.

"Shout for joy to the Lord, all the earth. Serve the Lord with gladness; come before him with joyful songs." Psalm 100:1, 2 (NIV).

God wants us to experience the joy of singing. A children's choir provides an opportunity for children to use their voices for His glory. And the words of the songs they sing serve as reminders of His love.

"Therefore go and make disciples of all nations ... teaching them to obey everything I have commanded you," Matthew 28:19, 20 (NIV).

God wants all of us to evangelize. A children's choir offers its members the chance to spread the Good News. When children obey God's command to tell others about Him, they feel a special blessing.

We've written this manual on working with a children's choir to encourage others to get involved, be more enthusiastic, find the task a little easier, and allow for more fun. But mostly we have written it in hopes that others can feel the love, joy, and care that we have known by becoming involved with God's children in this special way. We pray that the influence of our choir will be felt by the children for the rest of their lives and that they have drawn closer to God because of this experience.

When we first began, our choir, *Kids of the Kingdom,* we had no idea what it would come to mean to us, to the children and their families, and to the church itself. But then we all worked under such a handicap with our limited earthly vision. God must have known all along, though, for we have felt His love and care repeatedly ...

... through the children themselves. Their openness, willingness, and affection are addictive. The pleasure they

81

bring to others is immeasurable. And the joy of seeing individual choir members come to accept Jesus as their Savior is beyond description!

... through our congregation . They have been very supportive of the children's choir program. "Just love those 'Kids'!" we hear again and again. "What can we do to help?" we're asked. "Here's a little something extra for the choir," we're told as we're handed a donation. Members of the congregation have cut and sewn costumes, decorated for musicals, baked refreshments, made individual wooden Christmas ornaments for the children, built props, cut invitations and programs, and encouraged and supported the choir continuously. Several new members have told us they chose to join our congregation because they visited one Sunday when the children sang—or they heard about the choir—or they saw a musical—and they wanted their children to have a part of this Christian experience.

... through members of our community as they have become involved in our endeavors. We have been provided with opportunities to sing at the local mall, hospitals, TV stations, nursing homes, and other churches. The newspaper has printed articles and pictures before the musicals. Businesses have donated discontinued cabinets for our storage purposes and remnants of fabric for our costumes.

... within our respective families. Each of our children has been a member of the choir, and those who have "graduated" (after sixth grade) have become our prize assistants. And our husbands have never wavered in their support and encouragement (even on nights when the dinner table has been covered with construction-paper hearts instead of meat and potatoes).

... in our working relationship. When one of us is "down," the other is generally "up." When one of us is devoid of an idea, the other is usually full to the brim. Our friendship has grown and deepened. God has led us to draw deep within ourselves for talents and abilities we didn't know existed.

And God has been there all along. We have seen Him in the changes we've witnessed in some of the children. We have seen Him in the smiles and tears of senior citizens as they were touched by the children's singing. And we have seen Him in the ways things always seemed to "show up" when they were needed or "work out" when it seemed impossible.

We're thankful to have had the privilege of working with the childrens choir. It's been an exciting, fun, stimulating, sometimes tiring, enriching, broadening, and religious experience.

Will we always direct a youth choir? Nothing is forever except God! We will pray for His guidance and seek to do His will. God bless you as you, too, perform this special area of service as directors of children's choirs.

Notes:

84

Ideas

for Invitations and Programs

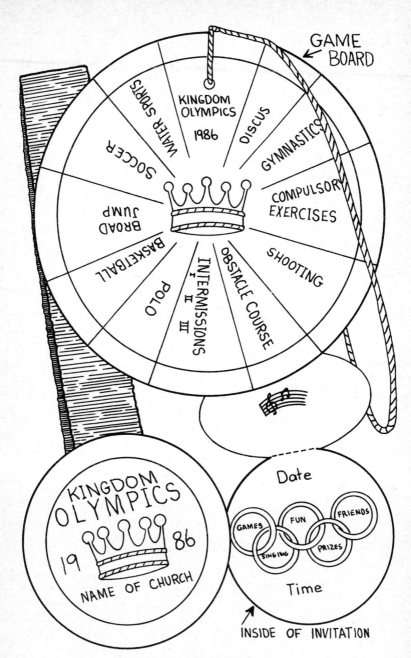

GAME BOARD

KINGDOM OLYMPICS 1986

DISCUS

GYMNASTICS

COMPULSORY EXERCISES

SHOOTING

OBSTACLE COURSE

INTERMISSIONS I II III

POLO

BASKETBALL

BROAD JUMP

SOCCER

WATER SPORTS

KINGDOM OLYMPICS 19 86

NAME OF CHURCH

Date

GAMES SINGING FUN PRIZES FRIENDS

Time

INSIDE OF INVITATION

Round-Up Invitations

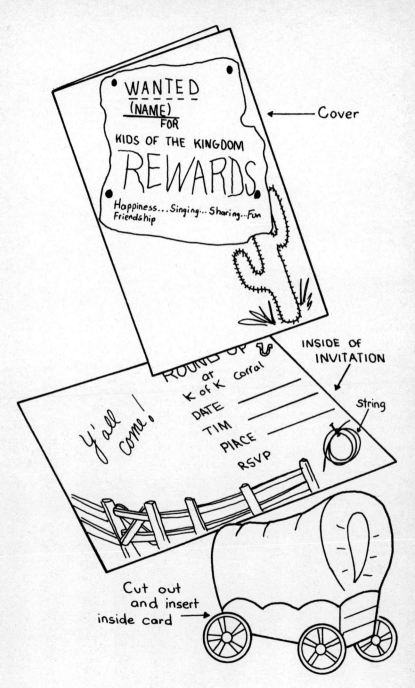

Cover

WANTED
(NAME)
FOR
KIDS OF THE KINGDOM
REWARDS
Happiness...Singing...Sharing...Fun
Friendship

INSIDE OF
INVITATION

String

ROUND UP
at
K of K Corral
DATE ____
TIM ____
PLACE ____
RSVP

Y'all come!

Cut out
and insert
inside card

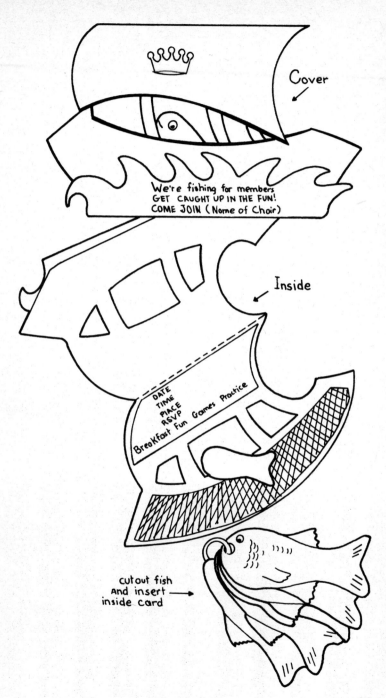

Cover

We're fishing for members
GET CAUGHT UP IN THE FUN!
COME JOIN (Name of Choir)

Inside

DATE
TIME
PLACE
RSVP
Breakfast Fun Games Practice

cutout fish
and insert →
inside card

**For the
Bulletin
Board**

Children's choir practice will be held every Saturday, beginning _____ (date and time).

The choir will present a song the first Sunday of every month during worship.

We have plans for Christmas and spring musicals.

Questions? Call _____ Directors' names and phone numbers

Hope to see **YOU!**

Invitations to Programs

come
with
US

to the
Promised Land

WHAT
WHERE
WHEN

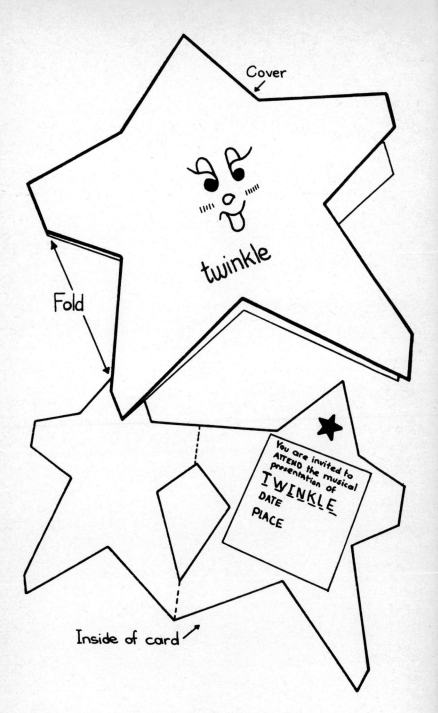

Cover

twinkle

Fold

You are invited to
ATTEND the musical
presentation of
TWINKLE
DATE
PLACE

Inside of card

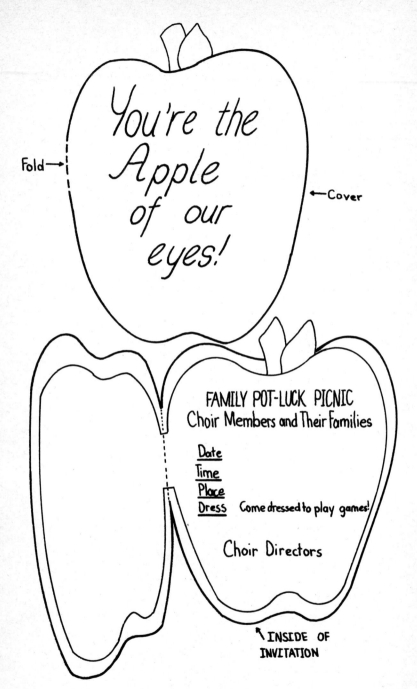

Fold →

← Cover

FAMILY POT-LUCK PICNIC
Choir Members and Their Families

<u>Date</u>
<u>Time</u>
<u>Place</u>
<u>Dress</u>   Come dressed to play games!

Choir Directors

↑ INSIDE OF
INVITATION

93

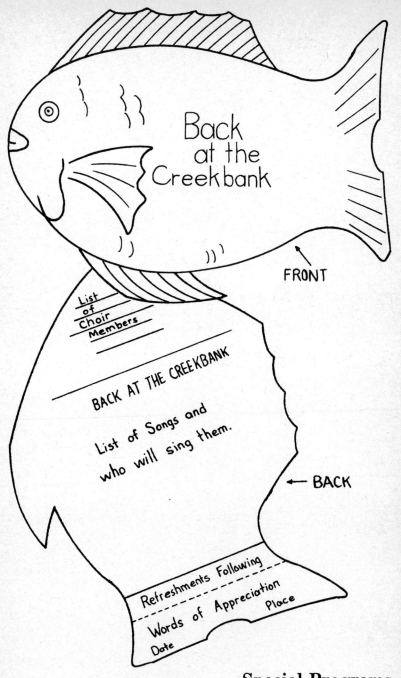

Back at the Creekbank

FRONT

List of Choir Members

BACK AT THE CREEKBANK

List of Songs and who will sing them.

← BACK

Refreshments Following

Words of Appreciation

Date   Place

Special Programs

FRONT COVER

DOWN BY THE CREEK BANK

PAPER BAG

PRESENTED BY
KIDS OF THE KINGDOM
Place
Date

Names of children in choir

BACK

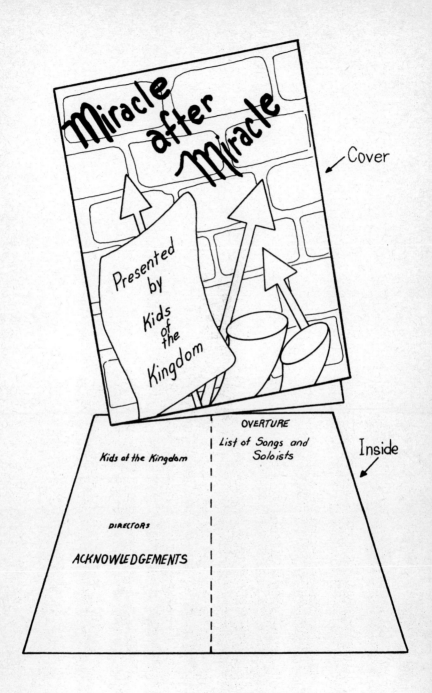

Cover

Miracle after Miracle

Presented by Kids of the Kingdom

Kids of the Kingdom

DIRECTORS

ACKNOWLEDGEMENTS

OVERTURE

List of Songs and Soloists

Inside